MILLBROOK ARTS LIBRARY

CRAFTS
FOR
DECORATION

edited by
Caroline Bingham
and Karen Foster

The Millbrook Press
Brookfield, Connecticut

Copyright © 1993 Merlion Publishing Ltd
First published in the United States in 1993 by
The Millbrook Press Inc.
2 Old New Milford Road
Brookfield, Connecticut 06804

Contributors:
Margaret Crush
Amanda Duncan
Heather Kingsley-Heath
Alison Leach

Designers: Jane Brett
            Tracy Carrington
            Roger Fletcher
Cover designer: Tracy Carrington
Picture researcher: Claire Allen
Typesetting coordinator: Gina Brierley

Printed and bound in Great Britain

Library of Congress Cataloging-in-Publication Data

Crafts for decoration/Caroline Bingham, Karen Foster, editors.
    p. cm. – (Millbrook arts library)
    Includes bibliographical references and index.
    Summary: Discusses how different cultures use color, natural materials,
and textures for making decorations. Hands-on activities include designing a
necklace, modeling a pot, tie-dying, letter decoration, and stenciling.
    ISBN 1-56294-098-8 (lib. bdg.)
    1. Handicraft – Juvenile literature. 2. Decoration and ornament – Juvenile
literature. [1. Handicraft. 2. Decoration and ornament.] I. Foster, Karen,
1964–   . II. Series.
TT160.C73 1993
745.594–dc20
                                            92-42945
                                               CIP
                                               AC

Artwork on pages 13 and 38 by Andrew Midgeley.

Models on pages 9, 13, 31, 35 and 39 by Jane Brett; pages 28/29
by Tracy Carrington; pages 23, 33 and 41 by Paul Fielder and page
15 by Sybil Gardener.

Photographs on pages 4/5, 6/7, 9, 10/11, 13, 15, 16/17,
18/19, 23, 26/27, 28/29, 31, 33, 35, 36, 39, 41 and 42/43
by Mike Stannard.

CONTENTS

Colors on fabric 4

Icat 6

Printing pictures on fabric 8

Tapestries...10

Embroidery 12

Appliqué 14

Decorating clay 16

Glazing clay 18

Color and patterns in wood 20

Glass pictures..22

Enamel work 24

Jewelry 26

Ancient Egyptian jewelry.................................28

Beads..30

Metallic decorations 32

Painted decorations...34

Stenciling..36

Decorative letters 38

Colors on paper 40

Making a clay pot 42

Learning a craft 44

Index...46

Acknowledgments..48

Colors on fabric

Imagine a world without color. It would be very dull indeed. Color brightens up the clothes we wear, the furniture we use, and the homes we live in. Objects made by craftspeople sometimes need brightening up, too. They are often made from natural materials – woods, clays, fabrics, and metals. Often color is added as an attractive decoration.

There are many different ways to add color to handmade objects. Glazes can be used to decorate clay, enamels to decorate metal, and dyes to color fabric. On this page we will look at some of the ways fabrics can be colored with dye.

A piece of batik cloth

Dye

Chemical dyes were invented in Europe in the 1850s, and soon they were being manufactured in factories all over the world. Before that time, all dyes were made by squeezing colored liquid out of natural materials such as berries, flowers, leaves, and even some small animals.

Many people still use natural dyes to color fabrics today. A substance called a mordant is added to the dye to bind it and the fabric together. Salt, lemon juice, and vinegar can all be used as mordants. Different mordants are used to make different shades of a dye color. The picture on the left shows one method of dipping fabric in dye that is used in Africa. The huge dye pits are lined with clay to make them waterproof, and are large enough to dye a long piece of fabric all at once. Large woven lids are used to cover the pits when they are not in use.

This man is dipping cloth into a dye pit in Nigeria

A batik artist in West Bengal

atik

pattern has been made on this piece
f fabric by creating areas on the fabric
at the dye cannot reach. One way of
oing this is to use a substance called a
esist. A resist is something like hot wax,
ce paste, or mud that is painted onto
ertain parts of the fabric and stops
he dye from reaching these
aces. Hot wax is used as a
esist in batik. Batik
rtists use a

A t'junting

hollow
tool called
a t'junting and
a brush to draw a
design onto the fabric
with the wax. When
the wax has hardened,
the fabric is dipped into
a colored dye. The process can
e repeated again and again, applying
yer after layer of wax and different
olored dyes. When the design is
nished, the fabric is ironed or boiled.
his melts and removes the wax. The
bric is then spread out to dry.

Tie-dyed fabric

Tie dye

Tie dye is the name of another craft that
creates patterns on fabric. In tie dye,
parts of the fabric are bunched up and
tied very tightly with fine thread. The
whole fabric is then dyed. The dye will
not penetrate the area wrapped by
thread, or the tight folds of fabric.
To make a more complicated
effect, different parts of the
fabric are bunched
together and a second
colored dye used.
Gradually the
patterns and the
colors build up into
jagged stripes.

Icat

Over 3,000 years ago the center of the Asian trade in silk and cloth was a city called Bokhara. This ancient city was a busy place, full of trained craftspeople who belonged to craft groups called guilds. Each guild produced its own special kind of cloth, and all the guilds made sure their members were highly skilled by making them pass a series of tests before they could join.

Bokhara was especially famous for producing woven pieces of silk called icat. Some lengths of icat are shown on these pages. Look at the blurred and fuzzy edges of the patterns.

Weaving icat in Ind

Pieces of icat

How icat is made

All cloth is made by weaving together
two sets of threads. The warp threads
run lengthways, while the weft threads
run from side to side. We have already
seen how cloth is dyed. For icat, only the
warp threads are dyed, which means
they have to be dyed before the cloth is
woven. They also have to be dyed in
patches, to form the pattern.

Simple bands of color are made by
bunching the threads together and tying
sections tightly with thread or strips of
rubber to prevent the dye from touching
these parts. When the warp threads have
been dyed, they are stretched onto the
loom. The weft thread is then woven
across the warp threads to create the
cloth. The patterns take on a fuzzy look
because the threads spread out slightly
when they are woven.

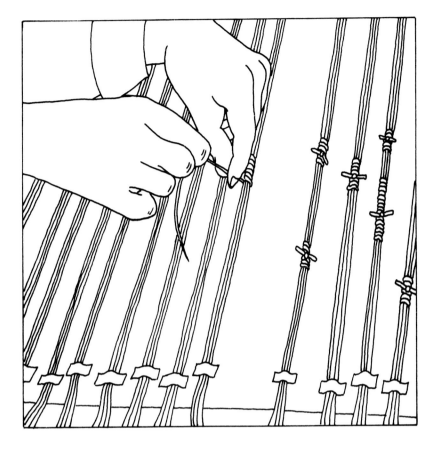

Preparing warp
threads to be dyed
for icat weaving

Fruit and flowers

Patterns such as these are complicated
to make, and yet, thousands of years ago,
the craftspeople of Bokhara were
producing intricate and beautiful
designs based on fruit, flowers, animals,
and insects. And each year they created
new designs and new colors!

Today, Bokhara is no longer such a well-
known center for weaving. But icat is
now a popular craft in many parts of the
world and beautiful icat patterns are
often seen on cotton cloth made for
clothes and furnishings.

Paṭolā weaving

A similar technique to icat was used in
India from the 1100s to produce paṭolās.
A paṭolā was a special silk sari that
formed part of the gifts given to a girl
before her marriage. Paṭolā designs were
as intricate as those produced by the
craftspeople of Bokhara many hundreds
of years before. They included birds and
flowers, elephants and dancing girls, all
set on a diamond-patterned
background.

Printing pictures on fabric

We have already looked at some of the ways in which dye is used to color thread and fabric. Other crafts use ink and paint to color fabric. One of these is silk-screen printing. This is a form of printing in which a design is cut out of a piece of paper called a stencil and laid on top of the fabric. Ink or paint is forced through a piece of silk that has been stretched across a screen. The ink colors only the area of fabric not masked by the stencil.

The women pictured below are using a screen to print a butterfly design onto fabric. The fine mesh of the screen prevents the ink from passing through too quickly and blotting onto the fabric beneath. The ink is pushed through the screen with a rubber blade, or squeegee. The women work on a long table, which means they can print several yards of fabric, leave that section to dry, and go on to the next. A clean screen is used for each different color.

These women are using a screen to print a length of fabric in Botswana

lock printing

an you think of a way of using blocks of ood to print designs onto fabric? The an pictured here is doing just this. lock printing is a craft that has been sed in India for many hundreds of ears. To make a block print, one urface of a block of wood has to be arved to produce a raised pattern. This urface is covered with ink and laid onto e fabric to be printed. The fabric rinter on the right is tapping the block make sure it has left an even print. He ill then lift it up, replace the ink and se it to print again. A whole length of bric can be printed by placing the ocks side by side. Like screen printing, ach new color used needs a clean ock.

This man is using a wooden block to print fabric

An Indian printing block

A printing block can also be made by attaching various materials to a wooden block to form a raised printing surface. Adding nails, string, dried beans, and cardboard are just a few ways texture can be added to the block. This Indian block has been made by hammering fine strips of copper onto the flat surface of the wood. It can be used to print a pattern of very fine lines because the ink touches only the very narrow edges of the metal strips.

Indian printing block

Make a block print

ake your own printing blocks by gluing ring to the smooth sides of different locks of wood. When the glue has ried, spread some ink on one of the aised designs with a sponge. Press the lock onto a piece of paper to print. ake sure you clean the block or use a ew block each time you want to add a ifferent color to your design. You can se the same idea with fabric paints nstead of ink to decorate a plain T-shirt.

Tapestries

Can you imagine what it would have been like to live in a huge castle 600 years ago? All the walls and floors of European castles were made from stone. The echoing rooms would have been very cold and drafty in bad weather! The inhabitants often tried to keep in the warmth by covering the walls with large woven pictures called tapestries. Tapestries added color and interest to a room, too.

Many beautiful tapestries were made in France and Flanders in the 1500s and 1600s. The weavers often worked from line drawings called cartoons, drawn by famous artists like the Italian painter Raphael. The Flemish city of Arras became so famous for the tapestries made there, that for a long time the word "arras" was used to mean "tapestry." Tapestries of this time were usually detailed pictures of stories from the Bible or from mythology. These smaller tapestries would have been used to decorate a wall, just like a painting.

Woven pictures

In a tapestry, the horizontal, or weft, threads completely cover the vertical, or warp, threads. This is different from ordinary weaving, where both sets of threads are visible. A tapestry weaver works from the back of the tapestry, using a sketched design, called a cartoon, as a guide.

Falconry was woven in the 1400s

The Lion is part of *The Forest* tapestry, woven in 1887

A woolen lion

The cartoon for this tapestry was drawn by the English craftsman William Morris in 1887. The tapestry was hand dyed and woven. If you take a quick glance at the lion, it is hard to believe that it has been formed from stitches! Look at the mane and the bristles on the lion's face. The detail of the weaving and the shades of the wool make it look as if it has been painted rather than sewn.

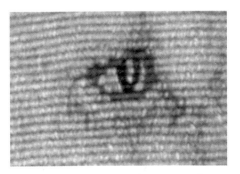

This picture shows the details of the lion's eye

Embroidery

The women pictured on this page are gathered together at a center for developing crafts and skills, situated in Bangladesh. They are enjoying one of the most popular crafts, embroidery. Embroidery has been used for thousands of years to decorate everyday clothing and furnishings, as well as special garments for occasions such as festivals and weddings.

These women are embroidering fabric at a crafts workshop in Bangladesh

This Chinese robe was embroidered in the 1700s

A special robe

This Chinese silk robe was embroidered about 300 years ago. The intricate patterns of birds and flowers are composed of thousands of tiny stitches. The robe has a simple shape, but the rich embroidery has made it very special. It is special in another way, for the pictures chosen each have a meaning. The curly lines at the bottom represent the sea. Sometimes this shape symbolizes clouds. Above the sea cranes are flying. These birds symbolize high official position, long life, and wealth.

Stitches and threads

The Chinese robe has been worked in perfect flat stitch using silk thread. This is just one of 300 different stitches, each of which has its own name. They fall into four basic types, as you can see in the diagrams on the right. The variety of stitches is useful because it means embroiderers can vary their designs by using different combinations of stitches. They can also choose from many different threads. The fibers that are chosen for the thread will depend both on the design and on what is available. Silk, cotton, linen, wool, and even metallic threads of gold and silver are all suitable for embroidery.

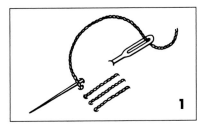

1. flat stitch

2. chain stitch

3. knot stitch

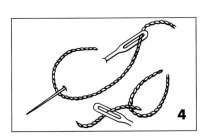

4. looped stitch

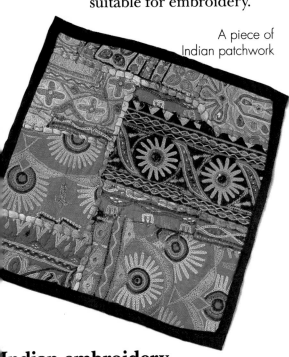

A piece of
Indian patchwork

Indian embroidery

This Indian patchwork of embroidery is in a completely different style from that shown by the Chinese robe. It is worked in cotton thread on cotton cloth. The fine lines of stitches are chain stitching. The center of the flowers holds tiny pieces of mirror called mica. Traditionally, these were used as a protection against evil spirits. The pieces of embroidery have been stitched together to make a cushion cover.

Design an embroidery

Embroidery designs are usually drawn onto a backing cloth, which may then be stretched over an embroidery frame. Draw a design for a piece of embroidery. You will need to decide whether you are designing a simple pattern that might be used as a mat, or a complicated pattern to decorate a special costume. Now look back at the embroidery stitches on this page. You can copy these stitches to work your embroidery. For example, the petals of a flower can be sewn with satin stitches or chain stitches, and the center of a flower with knot stitches.

Appliqué

Many Dutch and English people crossed the Atlantic Ocean in the 1700s and 1800s to settle in America. They were unable to take many possessions with them, and at times their life in a strange, new country must have seemed bleak and colorless. They needed cheap ways to decorate and furnish their homes, and they soon began to make use of a craft that was already popular in Europe at that time, called appliqué. Appliqué is the craft of stitching pieces of scrap fabric onto cloth to make unusual and colorful patterns. The American quilt shown below is decorated with appliqué. Fabric printed with birds or flowers was often cut up and used in this way.

This appliqué wall hanging was made in Nigeria

This appliqué quilt was made in America in the mid-1800s

Methods of appliqué

Appliqué is now popular throughout the world and a number of different methods are used. Simple shapes were stitched onto a dark background to make the Nigerian wall hanging pictured opposite. Embroidery can be added to give appliqué extra texture. Some appliqué is stuffed with padding, called wadding, to make a raised pattern. The people in the San Blas Islands, off the coast of South America, use reverse appliqué to make a type of cloth like the one below, called a mola. Layers of colored cloth are laid in a pile and the pattern is cut away to show the colors underneath. The edges of the fabric are then turned under and stitched.

Cut an appliqué picture

Trace a simple outline, such as an animal shape, onto a piece of fabric. It might help to look at the Nigerian wall hanging for ideas. Cut out your shape and pin it onto a larger piece of fabric, neatly turning under the edges. Stitch around the shape. Add other shapes to the piece of fabric in the same way. When you have finished, hang your appliqué on the wall or make a cushion cover from it.

A mola from the San Blas Islands

Decorating clay

Working clay into shapes – the craft of pottery – is one of the most ancient crafts known today. When it was first used, clay must have seemed like a magical substance! In its natural state, straight from the ground, it is soft enough to be shaped and molded into almost any form. Then, when it is heated, it hardens so that it is tough enough to be used as a carrying vessel or a cooking pot!

The smooth surfaces and flat color of a finished clay object are just right for decorating. The simplest way of doing this is to make marks on the clay before it is heated, or fired, and while it is still quite soft. The clay bowl shown here is 4,500 years old. The simple pattern was

A decorated vase from Ancient Greece

This English clay bowl was made 4,500 years ago

probably made by pressing a twisted cord into the wet clay. The decoration makes the pot look almost like a basket.

Painted decorations

The clay can also be painted with liquid clay mixed with natural colors or dyes. This mixture is called slip. The potter paints the slip onto the clay, just like an artist painting onto canvas. The Ancient Greeks used black and red slip that makes their painted pottery easy to recognize. The paintings often show scenes from everyday life, or from myths and legends. This vase is painted with a scene showing pots being decorated!

Today, potters have a wide variety of colors to choose from for slip. This modern bowl shows how beautifully colored slips can merge together to create soft designs to please the eye.

This bowl was made by an English potter called Amanda Duncan

Scratched patterns

Pots can also be dipped into slip to coat them completely in one color. Sometimes potters will use a sharp tool to scratch a design onto the slip before it dries. The design shows through in the color of the clay beneath.

The scratch technique is called sgraffito, and you can see an early example of it in the detail of a Mexican pot pictured below. Historians think the decorations on this pot are a form of ancient writing.

Detail of a Mexican pot decorated with sgraffito

Glazing clay

A clay pot is not waterproof, even if it is covered with slip. So potters developed a glossy liquid coating that would make their pots waterproof once they were fired. It is called glaze. Glaze undergoes a chemical reaction in the kiln and forms a hard, protective surface over the pot. The invention of glaze also created new kinds of decoration for pottery.

Early glazes

The earliest glazes we know of were used in Egypt about 2,000 years ago. The glaze was made from a mixture of sand and soda and, after being fired to quite a low temperature, it formed a brilliant turquoise color. This small bottle still shows some of its original glaze after all this time. You can imagine how bright it must have looked when it first came out of the kiln!

Today, potters have a wide variety of colored glazes to choose from. Some of these colors are shown in the glaze samples below. Did you know that most glazes are different shades of white before they are fired and that the color only develops in the kiln? Potters have to be very careful to label each glaze with its correct color.

This Egyptian bottle was glazed 2,000 years ago

Patterns on pots

Not all glazes are colored when fired. When potters have painted a design onto a pot with colored slip and allowed it to dry, they often glaze the pot with a layer of clear glaze. This seals in the design and gives the pot a glossy finish. Sometimes a pot is fired to harden it before the glaze is put on. This is called biscuit firing. The pot is then glazed and fired a second time.

This jug has a wax resist design

Using stencils

Paper shapes can be used as patterns to make glaze designs. The potter in the picture below has cut out a paper flower shape and is brushing colored glaze inside it. When she removes the paper, the flower shape is left as a glazed design on the pot.

Using a stencil to decorate a bowl

Resist designs

Stencils can also be used between coatings of glaze to make patterns. The paper acts as a resist, masking off an area that the glaze cannot penetrate. When the paper is peeled away, the pattern of the stencil is left in the original clay color. Wax painted onto clay gives a similar effect, although the wax is not removed. This modern jug shows a beautiful wax resist design.

Color and patterns in wood

Imagine picking up each of the wooden objects below. You turn them over and over in your hands, feeling the smoothness and comparing the rich colors of each. If you were a wood-carver about to begin a new carving, how would you decide which wood to use?

You might pick a wood with a rich, dark color – perhaps ebony. But if you wanted to create a carving with very intricate patterns, ebony would probably be the

The English wood-carver Grinling Gibbons carved this lace scarf

wrong choice, because it is a hard wood. It is better suited to making solid pieces of furniture than to detailed carving. The English wood-carver, Grinling Gibbons, chose limewood for his amazing carving of a lace scarf that you can see pictured above. Gibbons knew that limewood would be soft enough to carve into this delicate pattern and he was attracted by its light color. It is hard to believe that the scarf is made from wood and not real lace!

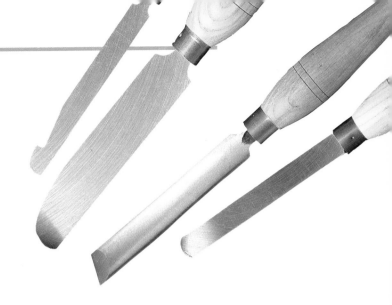

Natural patterns

Look again at the different kinds of wood on the previous page. Can you see the natural patterns on the surface of each object? These patterns are called the grain. They are formed as the tree grows outward in layers called rings. When the wood is sliced through, the rings can be seen as striped or wavy patterns over the surface.

Many craftworkers use the natural pattern of wood grain as a form of decoration when they carve. They are careful to cut the wood so that the best part of the grain will show. Then they use a tool with a rough edge, called a plane, to shave the wood until it is completely smooth.

A marquetry panel for a cupboard door, made in Italy in the 1520s

Finishing wood

When wood is finished, it means the surface has been protected and the beauty of the grain made to stand out. Woodworkers might use wax or clear varnish to finish wood. If they want to change the color of wood, they use a wood stain. This dyes the wood without hiding the grain.

Using several woods

This picture decorates a cupboard door. It is so realistic that it looks as if it has been painted on wood by a gifted artist. In fact, the picture has been made by a skilled woodworker using small pieces of different kinds of wood. Forming flat pictures with wood in this way is called marquetry.

To make a marquetry picture, the wood-carver first gouges out a shallow hollow with a sharp tool called a chisel. Small pieces of different woods are then cut out and arranged in the hollow to form a picture. They are carefully arranged so that their colors and grains create areas of light and shade in the picture. When the picture is complete, the pieces are glued in place. This panel has a perfect marquetry picture of a machine that is used to lift heavy objects, called a winch. You can see how cleverly the wood has been used to create a realistic picture.

Glass pictures

The stained-glass rose window in Chartres Cathedral, France

This magnificent stained-glass window is over 39 feet (12 meters) wide. It is situated in Chartres Cathedral in France and was created between 1203 and 1240. The cathedral has four of these huge windows, called rose windows because of their round shape, as well as 172 other stained-glass windows!

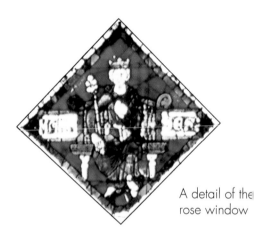

A detail of the rose window

Painting with light

At the time that these windows were made, most ordinary people could not read. Windows like these were placed in Christian churches as a form of "picture book," to teach people about their religion. Anyone could go into the church and "read" the stories illustrated in the glass pictures. As the people gazed in awe at the detail of these huge windows, light shining through from outside made the pictures glow with jewel-bright colors. Many people thought of the windows as something mysterious.

Almost a painting

In the 1400s, the way stained-glass windows were made began to change. Plain glass was covered with a liquid film of colored glass. When the film hardened, it could be scraped away to produce a picture or design. Stained-glass windows began to look more like paintings. Today, artists use both methods to make stained-glass windows. This picture shows a stained-glass maker in the process of cutting and fitting glass shapes. Many modern stained-glass windows are made to decorate rooms in private houses, shops, and offices.

Cutting stained-glass

How a rose window was made

First, the artist would make a full-size sketch of the finished picture or design. The pieces of colored glass were then cut out with a red hot iron. They had to be numbered or marked to help the artist remember where they fit. Then the artist painted details, such as faces, on the glass pieces and they were fired in a kiln. When they had cooled, the artist positioned the glass on the sketch. Finally, the pieces were joined with strips of lead that had to be melted, or soldered, together to hold the glass.

Most windows had to be made up in several panels because the whole structure was too heavy to support itself. Each panel was supported by an iron bar or delicate stone carving called tracery. Stone tracery supports the sections of the rose window pictured opposite.

Make a stained-glass picture

Draw a picture on tracing paper. You may need to draw a sketch first of all to plan the colors and shapes you want to use. Use a black crayon to draw heavily over the outline to make your lines of lead. These black lines should be about $1/4$ inch (6 millimeters) thick. Then use colored crayons to decorate your picture. The coloring needs to be quite neat. When you have finished, hang your picture against a window to make it glow. Try rubbing a tiny amount of cooking oil onto the back of the picture. This makes it even more translucent.

Enamel work

Bright colors

Cloisonné can be used to add color to vases, plates, jewelry – in fact to practically any metal object that can stand up to firing at temperatures up to about 1500°F (800°C)! It is these high temperatures that bring out an extra brightness in the colors of the enamel paints. This cloisonné elephant vase shows how colorful this decorative art can be.

This artist is applying enamel to the raised pattern of a cloisonné vase

This elephant vase was made about 400 years ago during the Ming dynasty

The artist in the picture isn't simply painting a metal vase. She is practicing a craft called cloisonné. In cloisonné, delicate metal strips are bent to follow a pre-marked design on the vase. The spaces between the metal strips are then carefully filled with brightly colored paints made from powdered glass called enamel. Wet enamel is dropped into place using a thin metal tool. The vase is then heated, or fired, to a very high temperature. This melts the wires and enamel onto the metal surface of the vase in a raised pattern.

...he three vases pictured below show the ...parate stages involved in the cloisonné ...chnique.

Thin strips of wire
mark the design

2. Enamel has been added
and the vase fired

3. The vase has been
polished

2

3

This painted enamel
bowl was made in
Russia in the late
1600s

...ainted enamel

...is possible to paint enamel directly
...nto a metal object, but the metal must
...rst be covered with a layer of white
...namel and fired. This richly
...ecorated Russian bowl has
...een painted on both sides
...sing this technique. The
...esign is scratched into the
...hite enamel with a needle
...nd then painted with one
...olor at a time. Each color
...as to dry before the next one
...added so that the colors do
...ot run into each other. It is a
...ow and careful process!

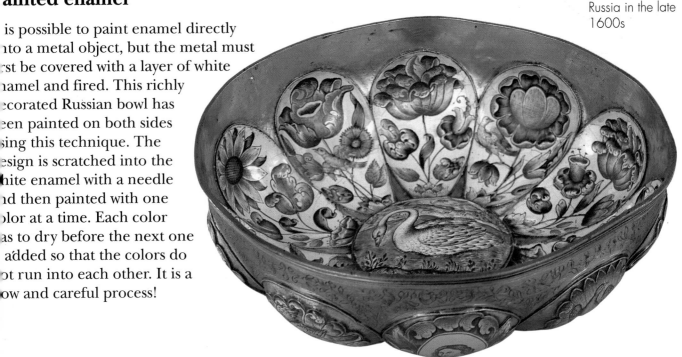

Jewelry

In prehistoric times, people made use of the natural materials around them to create simple jewelry. They made bracelets, earrings, and necklaces from shells, animal teeth, bone, and pebbles, stringing them onto leather thongs to decorate their bodies for rituals and celebrations. But while they were digging up roots for food or making tools, ancient people also found metals and gems under the ground or buried in rock. Imagine how exciting the discovery of a ruby or nugget of gold must have been thousands of years ago!

Gems

Gems are divided into precious and semi-precious stones. Precious stones are rare – they include diamonds, emeralds, pearls, and rubies. Semi-precious stones, like coral and quartz, have also been used in jewelry making for many thousands of years. Gemstones have a rough surface that is often cut and polished for jewelry. The person who does this is called a lapidary. You can see a picture of a lapidary at work on the right.

The shape, size, and color of a cut precious stone determines how valuable it will be. The largest cut diamond in the world is called the Star of Africa. It has 74 cut sides and is now in the Royal Sceptre of the Queen of England's crown jewels.

It is no wonder that gems, gold, and silver have been used to make jewelry. Their color, shine, or sparkle makes them a far more eye-catching form of body decoration than wood or bone. Gold, silver, and gems are also difficult to find, and this gives them a high value.

A lapidary

eating precious metals

n important change in the appearance
jewelry came about almost 5,500 years
o. Craftspeople discovered that
rtain metals, including gold and silver,
uld be heated over a fire, flattened
to thin sheets, then cut and shaped.
his crescent-shaped neck ornament,
lunula, was made over 4,000 years
o in Ireland. It shows how thinly
ated gold can be beaten. The
ecise decoration would have
en engraved by hand with a sharp
ol. At the same time, goldsmiths
scovered how to join pieces of
ecious metal together by melting,
soldering, them. This meant that
ry delicate pieces of jewelry could
made.

This Irish lunula was
made from gold
more than 4,000
years ago

is boy is making a filigree bracelet

Styles of jewelry

Jewelry changes in style according to
the fashions of the time. It can be as
simple as the Irish lunula, or as intricate
as the bracelet this boy is making. This
type of jewelry work is called filigree.
It involves twisting fine wires to produce
decorative shapes. It takes a long time to
master the skills needed to produce
filigree work.

Modern fashion jewelry includes
chunky plastic rings and string
necklaces. But most people agree that
jewelry made from
precious materials
and gems is the
most beautiful.

Ancient Egyptian jewelry

In 1922, a British archaeologist called Howard Carter discovered one of the most amazing collections of Ancient Egyptian objects ever found. He uncovered the tomb of a young Egyptian king, Tutankhamen, and inside discovered the largest single collection of gold and jewelry ever found.

Buried possessions

The Ancient Egyptians believed there was a life after death. When a king died, his body was preserved, wrapped in linen bandages as a mummy, and buried in a tomb. Possessions that the king might need in the afterlife were buried with him. Pieces of jewelry were considered to be especially important because many of them were lucky charms, or amulets, made to protect the wearer from evil spirits. The Egyptians also believed that gems had special powers and brought good luck, which was why Tutankhamen's mummy was covered with semi-precious stones.

Types of jewelry

Other archaeological finds and Ancient Egyptian paintings show us that the types of jewelry found in Tutankhamen's tomb were typical of all Egyptian jewelry. Semi-precious stones were set into gold to make necklaces, rings, and bracelets. Gold, believed by the Ancient Egyptians to be the metal of the gods, was heated and molded to form intricate and beautiful pieces of jewelry.

Ancient Egyptian scarabs

Wide bracelets decorated with symbols drawn from nature, and rings carved in the form of beetles, were also common. Carved beetles like the two pictured above were called scarabs. They symbolized the sun god, whom the Ancient Egyptians worshipped as the giver of life.

Egyptian necklaces
from the tomb of
Queen Shubad

Necklaces

The magnificent necklaces pictured above come from another Ancient Egyptian tomb, the tomb of Queen Shubad. They have the traditional Ancient Egyptian design that mixes beads and gold charms in repeated patterns. The beads are made from semi-precious stones like blue lapis-lazuli and red cornelian. Some beads were made from earthenware, which was glazed with bright colors.

The gold charms in the shapes of fish, insects, and birds all had special meanings. They were threaded between the beads in careful patterns. Can you see a scarab on one of the necklaces, too? We know that Queen Shubad would have worn four or five of these necklaces together, as well as rings, bracelets, ankle bracelets, and a headdress.

An Egyptian necklace to make

You can make your own Egyptian necklace using red, gold, and turquoise or blue paper. Cut the paper into long, thin triangles, and roll these up very tightly, beginning each time at the bottom of the triangle. You need to wrap the paper around a thin stick to make a hole in each bead. Dab a little glue on the paper as you finish rolling to hold it in position.

When you have enough beads, string them onto strong thread. You might like to add some wooden beads to your necklace. Make sure it is long enough to slip over your head, and knot the ends of the thread together. Now make a bracelet to match!

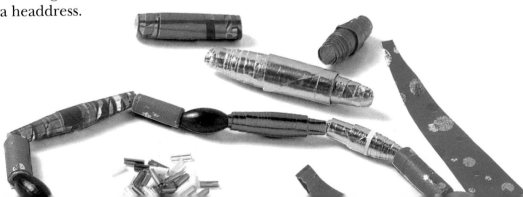

Beads

These wampum belts were woven by North American Indians from beads made from purple and white shells. Wampum belts were given and worn as signs of friendship, and their designs often symbolized important events. Later, the Indians exchanged the beaded belts or necklaces for goods from the European settlers who arrived in their country during the 1600s and 1700s. In the early 1700s, wampum came to be used as money in trade between the Indians and the settlers. Some Western Indians were still using wampum as money in the early 1900s.

Wampum belt

Uses of beads

In the late 1700s, the settlers began to give the Indians tiny glass beads, made by machine in Europe, in exchange for food and other necessities. The Indians used these beads to decorate clothes, shoes, and even woven baskets like the one in this picture. With more colors and different beads to choose from, the patterns became more complicated and interesting. Gradually, the Indians' use of the purple and white wampum beads decreased.

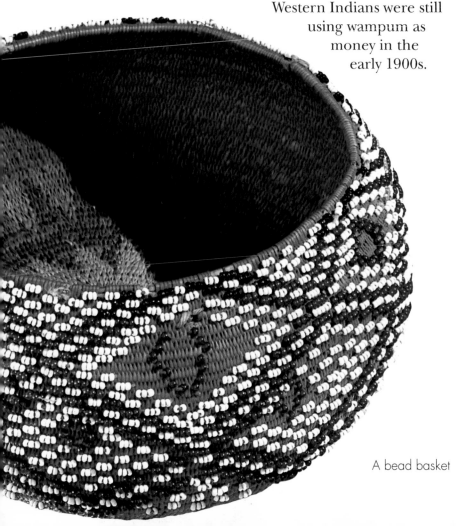

A bead basket

Beaded pictures

t around the same time, small glass eads were also being used to make ecorative knitted bead pictures in urope. Beaded pictures took a long me to make. Each bead's position had o be carefully planned on a pattern heet before knitting began. Fine bead nitting was used for purses, borders on onnets and shawls, and to make ecorated items like cushion covers.

Cherokee Indian bead weaver

How beads are woven

eads can be woven into decorated elts, necklaces, and bracelets. The eads have to be threaded onto the weft hread that runs across the fabric. The eft is then woven across the vertical, or arp, threads. A completed bead eaving looks like a neat sheet of beads ecause the thread is hidden inside the eads.

Try your own bead weaving

Bead weaving is simple to do, and you can experiment with making your own patterns. You will need lots of small glass beads. Make a loom by cutting nine grooves in two edges of a small cardboard box. The grooves should be the width of one bead apart. Then pass thin thread up and down the open side of the box using the grooves to hold the thread tight. This is your warp thread. String eight beads onto a long weft thread, and lay this string of beads across the warp threads. Each bead should fit into the space between two warp threads.

Now pass your needle and thread underneath the last warp thread and back up through the last bead. Then pass the needle underneath the next warp thread, and up through the next bead all across the row. String eight more beads onto your weft thread, and start the next row, then eight more, and so on. When your weaving is finished, fasten the weft thread and the ends of the warp threads with knots.

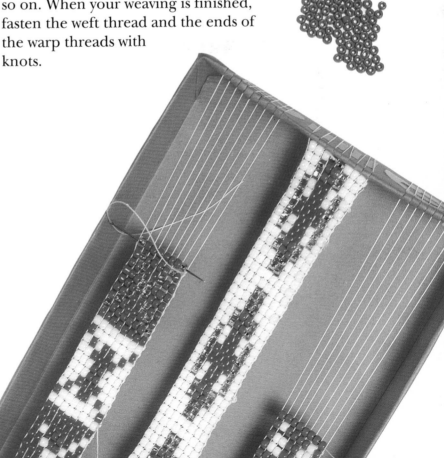

Metallic decorations

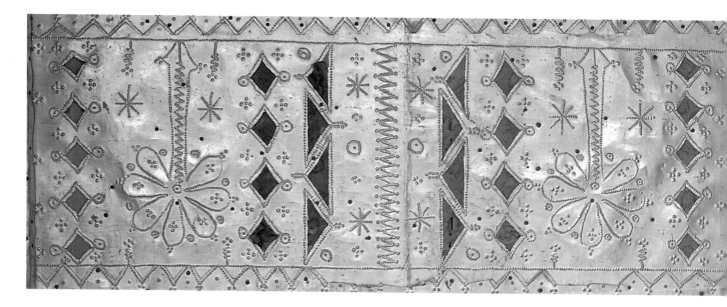

A section of a
Nigerian tin door

Most raw metals are hard and heavy –
they look too tough to mark in any way.
But, in fact, many metals are quite soft.
On page 27, we looked at one of the
ways in which gold can be decorated –
by engraving the surface with a sharp
tool. Pure gold is so soft that it cannot
be used on its own. It has to be mixed
with other metals, such as copper or
silver, to make it stronger.

Hammering designs

Soft metals can also be decorated with
hammered designs. Look at the tin
decoration on the detail of a door from
Nigeria, pictured above. A pattern has
been made on the wrong side of the tin
with a sharp tool and a hammer. This
method of decoration is sometimes
called embossing.

A blacksmith's workshop with forge, anvil,
and tools

These wrought-iron balconies decorate a house in New Orleans

Wrought iron

Most metals can be made into decorative forms once they have been heated. These finely made balconies in New Orleans are made from wrought iron. Craftworkers called blacksmiths make these decorative shapes by heating iron, then hammering it into twists or curls on a heavy object called an anvil. You can see an anvil in a blacksmith's workshop in the picture on the opposite page. The cone-shaped end of the anvil is used for shaping the curls. Patterns can also be made on the heated iron with a chisel. Railings, gates, and balconies used to decorate houses are often made from wrought iron.

A wrought-iron basket

Heating and shaping metal is a skilled craft which can be dangerous. For a safer alternative, you can make a wrought-iron-style basket with soft wire. You need to ask an adult to cut the wire into short lengths as you make the basket. Shape your first piece of wire into a circle. Now stretch four or five pieces across the circle, twisting the ends to secure them. This forms the base. You'll need to twist on eight upright wires to make the side of the basket, then attach another circle to the top.

Finally, twist two pieces of wire together, shape them into a semi-circle and attach this to the top as a handle. You can paint the basket with thick black paint for a more realistic wrought-iron effect.

Painted decorations

If you were faced with a dull surface such as a plain wall or a simple box, how would you decorate it? One of the simplest ways would be to paint it. Paints are liquid colors that can be brushed onto most surfaces. They provide a flat, bright coating of color that will brighten up even the most boring object.

This picture of a painted hut was taken in South Africa

Painted houses

Many people decorate the outside walls of their homes with paint. These decorations range from a simple coat o colored paint to cover wood or stone, t creative patterns like these decorations in different colors on the walls of this hut in South Africa.

A decorated Welsh
canal boat

Canal-boat painting

This picture of a Welsh boat shows a
form of painted decoration that has
become a tradition in England and
Wales. The tradition began when a
system of artificial rivers called canals
were built across the country in the
1800s to transport goods from factory to
factory. Special boats called narrow boats
were built to carry the goods, and many
of the canal workers lived on their boats.
Because these people were living among
dull, gray factories they began to paint
their boats with colored pictures and
designs to improve their surroundings.
Pictures of castles, flowers, and plants
were the most popular.

Canal painters had not been trained to
paint, and they used simple techniques.
They marked the design with chalk, and
mixed colors directly on the surface
being painted. Strong brush marks and
bright colors were a feature of canal
painting, and sometimes designs were
even painted with the fingers. Streaks of
white paint were used to add highlights.

A decorated can

You will need some thin paper patterned
with a design that you can cut out. Ask
an adult to give you a tin can that has no
sharp edges, clean the surface with
sandpaper, and coat it with black enamel
paint. When it is dry, glue your cut-out
pictures onto the can. Overlap the
pictures on the can as shown below.
When the glue has dried, add a coat of
varnish.

Stenciling

Painting large areas or objects with designs takes a long time. Imagine how long it would take you to paint an intricate design on the walls of your room! More than 1,000 years ago, the Chinese invented a quick, easy way to paint complicated patterns. They cut their designs out of thick cardboard or paper to make stencils.

If you wanted to paint a wall of your room using a stencil, you would place the stencil on the wall to be decorated and sponge over it with paint or ink. Lift the stencil away, and you will find a painted design. The stencil can be moved and the pattern repeated as often as necessary. It's a quick way to make painted decorations.

Stenciling in North America

Do you remember reading about the European settlers who took crafts like appliqué with them when they moved to North America? These people also made use of stencils. Stenciling bright designs onto the bare wooden walls of their new houses was another cheap, easy way to decorate their new homes, and the designs often reminded them of their old homes in Europe.

The settlers found that stenciling was an ideal way to add color to any kind of wood. They cut simple stencils such as the ones shown on the opposite page and painted over them with bright paint in red, yellow, and green, which they made from plant and vegetable dyes. They painted stencil designs on furniture – chairs, baby's cradles, blanket boxes, and tables – and on walls. It must have been hard to find a surface that wasn't decorated in some American homes! Stenciling was also popular in England, where stenciled wallpaper was used to decorate wealthy homes in the 1600s and 1700s. Stenciling is still a widely used craft, because it is a quick way of decorating objects.

A stenciled rocking chair

Decorative letters

The monks used a pen made from a feather, called a quill, and inks. Scribes wrote on paper called parchment that was made from animal skins. The scribes' handwriting was carefully formed and beautiful to look at.

The books the scribes wrote are called illuminated manuscripts. Manuscript means "written by hand." Illuminated is the word we use to describe the decoration – the pages were so brightly colored that they seem to shine with light. The monks used rich colors and even gold and silver leaf to decorate initial letters and margins. Often a complete miniature painting was painted into the initial letter, as is shown in this beautiful letter B.

In Europe before the 1400s, most ordinary people did not know how to write. Writing was thought of as a special craft, and it was taught only to carefully trained monks, called scribes. Scribes spent their time copying ancient writings into book form. They sat at high, sloping desks like the one in this picture.

This decorated letter B comes from a manuscript of the 1400s

A scribe at his desk

This Chinese boy is using a calligraphy brush

Calligraphy

Today, many people still practice the craft of writing beautifully. It is called calligraphy. Modern calligraphers can choose from an enormous variety of specially made pens, but many use a brush and ink. This is the method traditionally used by calligraphers in China, where calligraphy is an important part of everyday life. The Chinese brush has a bamboo handle and animal hair bristles which are shaped to a fine point.

Care and skill

No matter what the language, the calligrapher has to use slow, careful strokes to form each letter. The width and shape of the strokes depend on how the calligrapher changes the pressure and angle of the brush or pen. The calligrapher has to hold the brush with a steady hand. Spacing is also important in calligraphy. The space between each word has to be the same, and enough space must be left between different lines so that no part of a letter touches one on another line.

Decorate an initial

Decorate the initial letter of your name in the same way that scribes did 600 years ago. Draw the letter on a clean sheet of white paper. Use bright colors to add patterns and pictures. Try to tell a story or say something about yourself in your painting.

Colors on paper

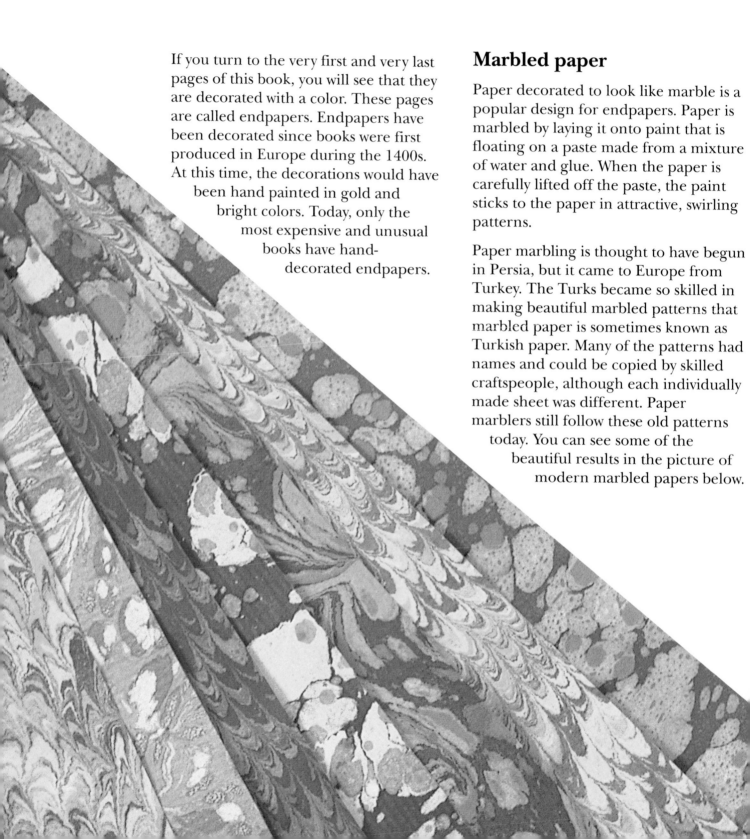

If you turn to the very first and very last pages of this book, you will see that they are decorated with a color. These pages are called endpapers. Endpapers have been decorated since books were first produced in Europe during the 1400s. At this time, the decorations would have been hand painted in gold and bright colors. Today, only the most expensive and unusual books have hand-decorated endpapers.

Marbled paper

Paper decorated to look like marble is a popular design for endpapers. Paper is marbled by laying it onto paint that is floating on a paste made from a mixture of water and glue. When the paper is carefully lifted off the paste, the paint sticks to the paper in attractive, swirling patterns.

Paper marbling is thought to have begun in Persia, but it came to Europe from Turkey. The Turks became so skilled in making beautiful marbled patterns that marbled paper is sometimes known as Turkish paper. Many of the patterns had names and could be copied by skilled craftspeople, although each individually made sheet was different. Paper marblers still follow these old patterns today. You can see some of the beautiful results in the picture of modern marbled papers below.

Combing the paint paste

Marble your own paper

You will need to dilute some oil paint with a little turpentine. Use a saucer to do this, and ask an adult to help. Then use a paintbrush to sprinkle drops of the diluted paint onto the surface of a large bowl of water. The paint will float. Swirl it around gently with the other end of the brush.

Wearing a pair of rubber gloves, hold a clean sheet of paper by the corners and lower it onto the surface of the water. Quickly lift it up, so that the paint sticks to the paper in swirling patterns. Make sure you keep the paper flat so that the paints don't run. Then leave it to dry. Experiment with different techniques. Try combing the paint across the surface of the water and using two or three colors.

Paste paper

Paste papers look similar to marbled paper, but they are made in a different way. Paste is mixed with powdered color and dabbed onto damp paper. Intricate raised patterns can then be formed when a brush or comb is pulled across the colors. Paste paper was often used to make endpapers in Germany in the late 1700s.

Making a clay pot

1. Wedging the clay

2. Opening out

3. Shaping the pot

Using the wheel

The potter then forms the clay into a ball and wets the underside so that it sticks to the wheel. The ball of clay must be placed as near as possible to the center of the wheel. Once the clay is centered, the potter uses her thumb to find the middle of the centered clay and then pushes it outward with her fingers. This is called opening out.

When a potter sets out to make a pot, she first has to choose and prepare the clay she is going to use. She pummels the clay to remove any air bubbles inside it in a process called wedging. If the air bubbles were left in, the clay might explode when it is heated.

1. Cutting the pot away from the wheel

2. Removing extra clay

3. Taking the pot out of the kiln

Now comes the difficult part! The potter squeezes the clay between her hands and pulls upward to form the basic shape of the pot. She repeats this action, starting from the base each time, until the pot is the right shape and the sides have an even thickness.

The pot is then cut off the wheel using a wire. Now the potter removes any extra clay from the base of the pot using a sharp tool called a turning tool. When the pot is nearly dry, or leather hard, it can be decorated using slip, which is colored liquid clay. This can be painted over a scratched design, as here. The pot is now left to dry completely then placed in an oven, or kiln, to be baked, or fired, for the first time. This first firing is called the biscuit firing.

Finishing the pot

Once the pot has cooled from the biscuit firing, a layer of a varnish called glaze is applied to the pot. The glaze can be poured or sprayed onto the pot, or the pot can be dipped into the glaze. The glaze is left to dry, then the glazed pot is fired for a second time. This hardens the glaze into its final form and color. When the pot is removed from the kiln, it is complete.

Painting on the slip

44

Learning a craft

Woodworking is
a popular craft

Have you made any of the craft objects
suggested in the activities in this book?
Most of these are fairly simple and don't
require special knowledge or equipment.

If you have particularly enjoyed making
one of the objects, you may decide you
want to learn more about the craft
involved.

Further learning

You may find that you have a particular talent for your chosen craft. Perhaps you will even want to make it your career! If so, there are college courses available so that you can spend three or four years specializing in an aspect of your craft before you start work. In the meantime, though, just enjoy any time you spend practicing your favorite craft and producing finished objects!

Stone carving is a difficult craft to learn

Working with clay can be fun!

Taking lessons

The best way to learn a craft is to take lessons from an experienced teacher. You may already have the opportunity to learn pottery or woodworking at school, or you may have to look for lessons you can take in your spare time. You will find that classes are often run at a school or craft center in your area and the teacher may be a local craftsperson.

Lessons will give you the opportunity to find out if you enjoy the craft you have chosen before you spend a lot of money on equipment. Basic materials are usually included in the price of your lessons. You will also be able to meet other people who enjoy that craft, too.

Index

A
Africa   4, 34
American Indian   30
American quilt   14
anvil   32, 33
appliqué   14–15
Arras   10
Asia   6

B
bamboo   39
Bangladesh   12
batik   4, 5
beads   29, 30–31
Bengal, West   5
biscuit firing   18, 43
blacksmiths   32, 33
block printing   9
Bokhara   6, 7
book   38, 40
Botswana   8

C
calligraphy   39
canal-boat decoration   35
Carter, Howard   28
cartoon   10, 11
castle   10
chain stitch   13
Chartres Cathedral   22
chemical dye   4
China   12–13, 36, 39
chisel   21
clay   16–19, 42–3
cloisonné   24–25
cloth   4–9, 14–15
coral   26
cotton   13
crown jewels   26

D
diamond   26
Duncan, Amanda   17
dyeing   4–5, 7, 16

E
ebony   20

Egypt, Ancient   18, 28–29
embossing metal   32
embroidery   12–13, 15
emerald   26
enamel   4, 24–25
endpapers   40, 41
England   11, 16, 20, 37
   canal-boat   35
   crown jewels   26
Europe   4, 14, 31, 40
   tapestry   10–11
   writing   38

F
fabric   4–9
   appliqué   14–15
   embroidered   12–13
   tapestry   10–11
Falconry (tapestry)   10
filigree   27
firing clay   43
Flanders   10
flat stitch   13
Forest, The (tapestry)   11
France   10, 22
furniture   37

G
gem   26, 28
Germany   41
Gibbons, Grinling   20
glass   22–23
   enamel   24
glaze   4, 18, 19, 43
gold   27, 28–29, 32
grain   21
Greece, Ancient   16
guilds   6

I
icat   6–7
illuminated manuscript   38
India   9, 13
Ireland   27
iron work   33
Italy   21

welry   26–29

iln   43
not stitch   13

pidary   26
ssons   44, 45
mewood   20
ion, The (tapestry)   11
oped stitch   13
nula   27

arbled paper   40–41
arquetry   21
etal   24, 25, 27, 32–33
Mexico   17
ola   15
ordant   4
Morris, William   11

arrow-boat decoration   35
ecklace   29
New Orleans   33
Nigeria   4, 14, 32
orth America   30, 37
orth American Indian   30

aint   34–35, 36–37
aper   40–41
archment   38
aste paper   41
atchwork   13
atola   7
earl   26
lane   21
otter   42–43
otter's wheel   43
ottery   16–19, 42–43
recious metal   27
recious stone   26
rinting block   9

uartz   26
uilt   14

Raphael   10
esist   5, 19
Rose Windows   22, 23

Royal Sceptre   26
ruby   26
Russia   25

S
San Blas Islands   15
scarab   28, 29
scribes   38
semi-precious stone   26
sgraffito   17
shell   30
Shubad, Queen   29
silk   6, 7
silk-screen printing   8
silver   27
slip   16, 17, 18
soldering   27
South Africa   34
stained glass   22–23
Star of Africa, The   26
stencil   8, 19, 36–37

T
tapestry   10–11
tie dye   5
tin   32
t'junting tool   5
Turkey   40
Turkish paper   40
Tutankhamen   28

V
varnish   21
vase   16, 24, 25

W
Wales   35
wallpaper   37
wampum belt   30
warp thread   7, 10
wax resist   19
weaving   7, 10, 31
wedging clay   42
weft thread   7, 10
West Bengal   5
wood   20–21
wood-block printing   9
wood carvings   20, 21
wood stain   21
wrought iron   33

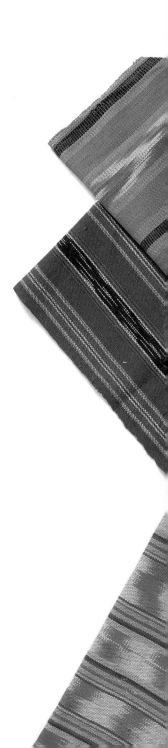

Acknowledgments

The publishers would like to thank the following for permission to reproduce these photographs:

The American Museum, Bath for appliqué quilt (page 14); bead basket (page 30) and stenciled chair (page 37). The Ancient Art and Architecture Collection for cloisonné vase (page 24); South African painted hut (page 34) and market (page 45). The Ashmolean Museum, University of Oxford for Ancient Greek vase (page 16). The Trustees of the British Museum for clay bowl (page 16); Mexican pot (page 17); painted enamel bowl (page 25); Irish lunula (page 27) and Ancient Egyptian scarabs jewelry (page 28). Cephas for bead weaver (page 31). Collections/Ben Boswell for stenciling a pot (page 19). Collections/Anthea Sieveking for boy learning pottery and boy learning stone carving (page 45). Compton Marbling for marbled paper (page 40). Craft Suppliers Ltd. for wooden objects (page 20) and tools (page 21). Amanda Duncan for earthenware bowl (page 17). Robert Estall for girl learning woodwork (page 44). Saraj Guha for forge (page 32). Michael Holford for Chinese silk robe (page 12); rose window at Chartres Cathedral (page 22); boy making a filigree bracelet (page 27); Egyptian necklaces (page 29) and wampum belts (page 30). Jacqui Hurst for icat weaving (page 50) and marbling paper (page 41). The Hutchison Library for Nigerian dye pit (page 4); making batik in West Bengal (page 5); screen printing in Botswana (page 8); embroidery in Bangladesh (page 12); Nigerian appliqué wall hanging (page 14); three stages in making a cloisonné vase (page 25); Nigerian tin door (page 32); decorated canal boat (page 35) and Chinese boy doing calligraphy (page 39). The MacQuitty International Photographic Collection for blockprinting (page 9); applying enamel to a cloisonné vase (page 24) and a lapidary (page 26). The Petrie Museum, University College, London for Egyptian bottle (page 62). The Board of Trustees of the Victoria and Albert Museum for *Falconry* tapestry (page 10); *The Lion* tapestry (page 11); carving by Grinling Gibbons (page 20) and marquetry panel (page 21). Sasha Ward for making stained glass (page 23). The Dean and Chapter of Winchester Cathedral for decorated initial B (page 38) and World Pictures for cast iron balconies in New Orleans (page 33).

The publishers would also like to give special thanks to Heather Kingsley-Heath and Gordon and Dorothy Whittle for the loan of items for photography and to Fiona Bates for advice and for allowing herself to be photographed for the book.